BATTLE OF MONS GRAUPIUS THE ROMANS BEAT THE PICTS
STIRLING CASTLE
WALLACE MONUMENT
TO THE HIGHLANDS
BANNOCKBURN WHERE ROBERT THE BRUCE BEAT THE ENGLISH
ABERDEEN
CARRON IRON WORKS
ALKLAND PALACE
SCONE
DUNDEE
DUNNOTTAR WHERE THE CROWN JEWELS WERE HIDDEN
DUNFERMLINE ABBEY FOUNDED BY ST. MARGARET
ST. ANDREWS
LINLITHGOW PALACE
LOCH LEVEN CASTLE WHERE MARY WAS FIRST IMPRISONED
FIFE WHERE ALEXANDER III FELL OFF HIS HORSE
FORTH BRIDGES
EDINBURGH
JAMES IV'S SHIP 'THE GREAT MICHAEL'
THE GIANT CANNON, MONS MEG IS NOW IN EDINBURGH CASTLE
ABBOTSFORD HOME OF SIR WALTER SCOTT
HADRIAN'S WALL
BATTLE OF FLODDEN FIELD WHERE JAMES IV WAS KILLED

The Story of SCOTLAND

Told by Richard Brassey and Stewart Ross
Illustrated by Richard Brassey

TED SMART

For my mother – RB

For Ander Henderson, stepfather and dear friend – SR

First published in Great Britain in 1999 by
Orion Children's Books/Dolphin Paperbacks
a division of the Orion Publishing Group Ltd
Orion House
5 Upper St Martin's Lane
London WC2H 9EA

This edition produced for
The Book People Ltd
Hall Wood Avenue
Haydock
St Helens WA11 9UL

A catalogue record for this book is available from the British Library

Printed and bound in Italy

ISBN 1 85881 667 X (HB)
ISBN 1 85881 549 5 (PB)

The land that is now Scotland was once a part of North America. Many millions of years ago, it broke away, bumped into Europe and stuck fast. The Atlantic Ocean opened up in between.

The dinosaurs came and went.

ANIMALS OF THE LAST ICE AGE

The Ice Ages buried Scotland under ice, two miles thick. Only after the ice had finally melted, about 8000 years ago, did the first people move in to hunt and gather food.

As time and generations went by the people learnt how to farm and build houses of stone.

They began making tombs and mysterious stone circles. By 2500 BC they were using copper for jewellery, tools and weapons.

The Stone Age village of Skara Brae in Orkney lay hidden for about 4000 years before a storm blew away the sand that covered it.

During the Bronze and Iron Ages, tribes gathered together into small kingdoms, often based around hilltop forts.

In about 80 AD, the Romans arrived. They built forts and roads over the Lowlands and marched into the Highlands. They called the people who lived there 'Picti', meaning 'painted ones'.

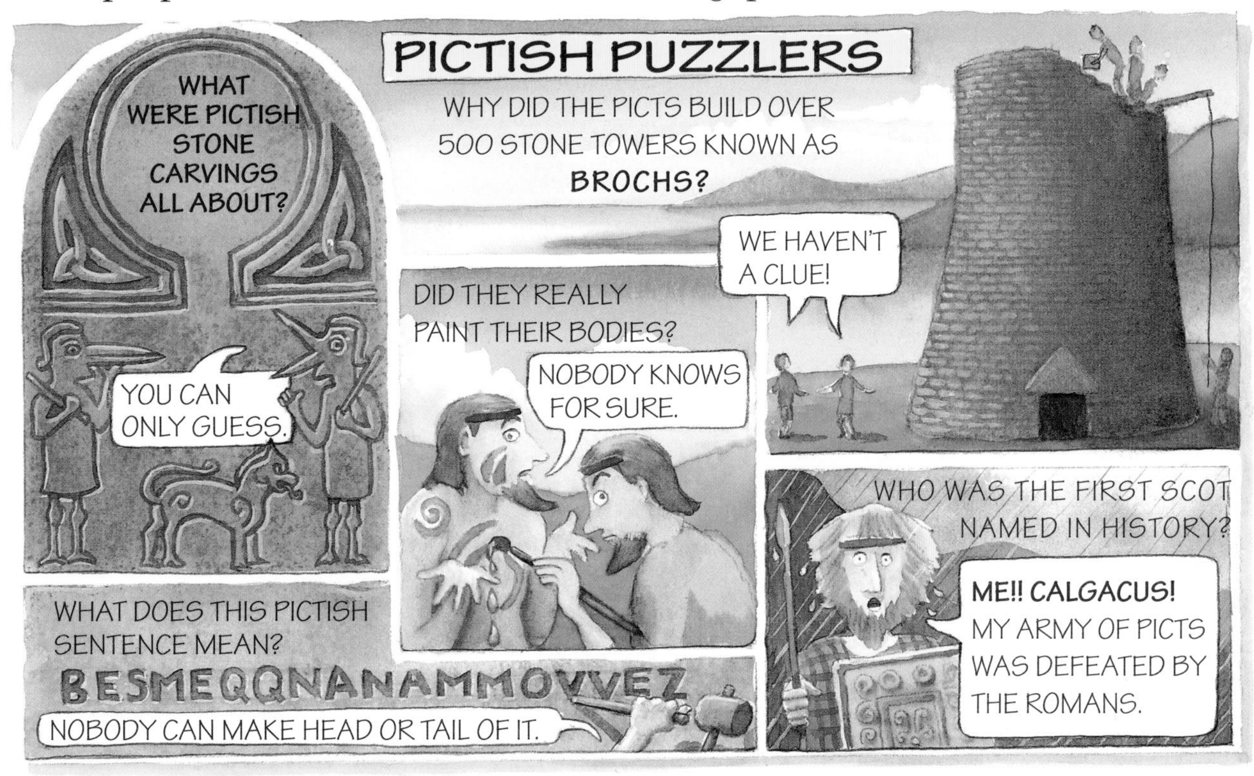

Although the Romans beat the Picts in battle, they were unable to conquer Pictland, so they decided to wall it off with the Antonine Wall (made of earth) and the much larger Hadrian's Wall (made of stone). After about 300 years they went back to Rome.

The Highland Picts and Lowland Britons were not left in peace for long. Scots sailed over from Ireland. Angles arrived from England. Meanwhile missionaries moved in and did their best to get the whole lot to become Christian.

Confused ...? So was everybody.

Things got even more complicated when the Vikings began moving in. But gradually, over the next few hundred years, the Scots came out on top. They created the Christian Kingdom of Scotland. From now on all the different people would be known as Scots ... except the Vikings!

TOP SCOT

KENNETH McALPIN DIED 858

Sometimes called the first King of Scotland. He was king of both Scots and Picts. He didn't have much success against the Vikings.

The Kingdom of Scotland took many years to settle down. The Vikings still held the north and west and there were frequent squabbles over who should rule the rest of the country. From time to time, war broke out with England. Some Scottish kings even had to accept the King of England as their lord.

MACBETH

Macbeth was one of the better early kings. Most of Shakespeare's famous play about him is inaccurate or made up.

Despite all this, the people were busier than ever. Towns grew up and merchants got richer. David I gave large amounts of land to knights from England and France. In return they helped him keep the peace. Scots got used to sorting out their arguments in law courts rather than by fighting.

Then in 1286, disaster ... Alexander III fell off his horse and died. The crown was up for grabs.

TOP SCOT ST MARGARET (1046–1093)

English-speaking Margaret married King Malcolm III nicknamed Canmore, meaning 'Great Chief' or 'Big Head'. She founded churches, encouraged learning and was later made a saint. He spoke Gaelic, could not read or write and liked nothing better than a good battle. Against all odds they loved each other madly.

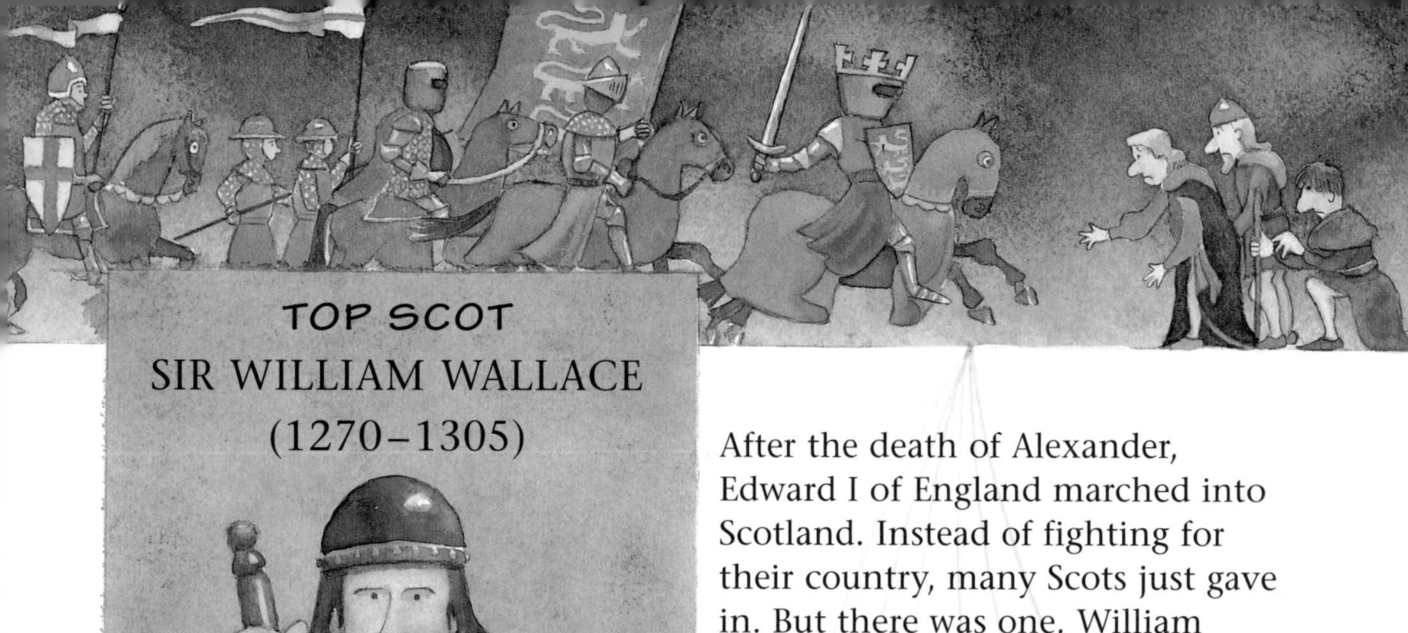

TOP SCOT

SIR WILLIAM WALLACE (1270–1305)

Perhaps Scotland's greatest hero – even though he was eventually defeated after the Battle of Stirling Bridge. He was captured by the English in 1305 and taken to London where he was hanged, drawn and quartered.

After the death of Alexander, Edward I of England marched into Scotland. Instead of fighting for their country, many Scots just gave in. But there was one, William Wallace, who fought back bravely and won a great victory at Stirling Bridge.

Nine years later Robert the Bruce became king. Bit by bit, he drove the English out and finally smashed them at Bannockburn (1314).

A famous story says Robert the Bruce got hope in his struggle against the English by watching a spider trying to fix its web to a beam. The spider triumphed after six attempts – and so did the Bruce.

The English also tried to get rid of Bruce's son David, but he hung on and left the throne to his nephew Robert – the first of the Stewart kings.

The first Stewarts could barely keep control. Robert III even tried to send his son, Prince James, to France for safety. Unfortunately James was captured by pirates and spent the first eighteen years of his reign as a prisoner in England.

THE FEEBLE FIRST STEWARTS

ROBERT II
– known later as 'Old Bleary' – ended up too doddery and decrepit to rule properly.

ROBERT III
A kick from a horse left him lame and depressed. The shock of James's kidnapping finished him off.

ARE YE A WORLDLY CREATURE OR HEAVENLY THING?

James I fell in love with his future wife Joan Beaufort when he saw her from his prison window. He even wrote a poem about her.

The foundation of the University of St Andrew's in 1412 shows that early Stewart history was not all chaos and war.

James II used the giant cannon Mons Meg to bring the nobles to heel.

The Stewart rulers were an unlucky lot (see opposite page). Even so, the country did well under their government. They took control of the Western and Northern Isles and worked hard to get the nobles and Highlanders to obey them.

THE HIGHLANDERS

The Highlanders lived in the rugged and remote glens of the north-west. Most belonged to a clan – a group of families, usually with the same name. They were often keener on their clan than their king, which really annoyed the Stewarts.

The population rose to about half a million. There were more universities than in England. All well-to-do young men studied law, the arts and Latin. Poetry flourished and many beautiful books were published.

New castles and tower houses were built and old ones improved. Fine ships sailed from Scottish shipyards. Scots engineers were in demand from Dublin to Moscow.

BABY KINGS AND STICKY ENDS

Most of the Stewarts met sticky ends so their children were very young when they came to the throne. Unhappy squabbles usually followed.

JAMES I

13

Stabbed

JAMES II

6 Killed by an exploding cannon

JAMES III

8

Stabbed

TOP SCOT

JAMES IV

15

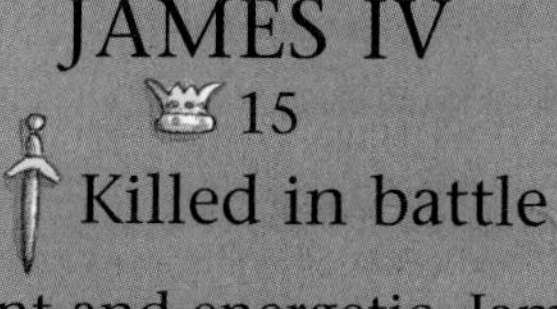

Killed in battle

Intelligent and energetic, James was Scotland's most exciting king. He felt guilty that he had rebelled against his father and wore an iron belt to remind him of his sin. As he got older, he added new links. He said they stopped him forgetting his murdered Dad but without them he would have burst.

JAMES V

1

Died of misery aged 30

MARY QUEEN OF SCOTS

1 week

Executed

[see page 14]

JAMES VI

1

Died of old age!!!

[see page 16]

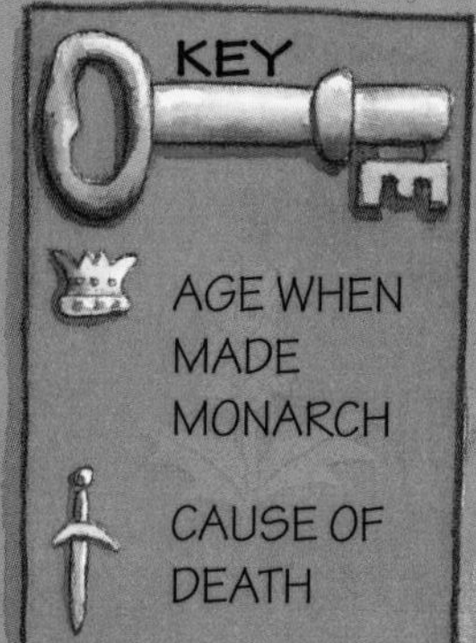

AGE WHEN MADE MONARCH

CAUSE OF DEATH

When Mary became Queen as a tiny baby, England's Henry VIII attacked Scotland to force her to marry his son … who was five.

The plan failed. Mary married a French prince instead and for a year she was queen of Scotland and France. Then her husband died and she returned to Scotland.

PREACHER JOHN KNOX was willing to tell anyone – even Queen Mary – that the Protestants were right and the Catholics wrong.

During Mary's reign Scotland changed from a Roman Catholic to a Protestant country. Fine Catholic monasteries and abbeys were plundered and the nobles helped themselves to their lands. Mary remained Catholic, which added to her problems.

TARTAN

Scotland's famous patterned cloth is a modern version of traditional highland dress.

THE STORY OF MARY QUEEN OF SCOTS

MARY WAS SENT TO FRANCE AS A SMALL GIRL AND GREW UP THERE. WHEN SHE WAS SIXTEEN, SHE MARRIED THE FRENCH PRINCE FRANCIS. HE DIED TWO YEARS LATER SO SHE CAME BACK TO SCOTLAND.

SHE WAS LIVELY AND BEAUTIFUL AND LOVED TO RIDE HORSES.

SHE ALSO LOVED PARTIES AND HATED IT WHEN JOHN KNOX TOLD HER NOT TO HAVE FUN.

SHE HAD TWO SCOTTISH HUSBANDS.

LORD DARNLEY WAS MURDERED AFTER 18 MONTHS.

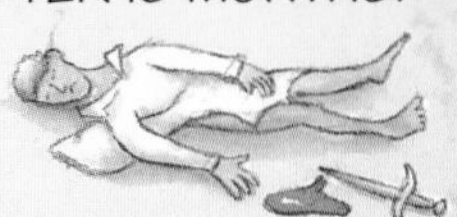

THE EARL OF BOTHWELL RAN AWAY AFTER A FEW WEEKS.

SHE ANNOYED ALMOST EVERYONE OF IMPORTANCE, SO SHE WAS LOCKED UP IN A CASTLE AND HER CROWN TAKEN AWAY. BUT SHE MANAGED TO ESCAPE TO ENGLAND.

HER COUSIN, QUEEN ELIZABETH I, THOUGHT MARY WAS PLOTTING TO STEAL THE THRONE OF ENGLAND FROM HER. SHE KEPT MARY SHUT UP IN DRAUGHTY CASTLES AND COUNTRY HOUSES.

ELIZABETH THOUGHT MARY SUCH A NUISANCE, THAT IN THE END SHE ORDERED HER HEAD TO BE CUT OFF.

James VI was only one when his mother, Mary, escaped to England. Others governed until he was old enough to take over. A clever, peace-loving man, he then ruled Scotland better than any king before him.

In 1603 he became king of England as well. After this he lived in England and returned to Scotland only once.

To keep troublesome Ulster Catholics under control, James 'planted' thousands of Protestant Scots there. The problems this caused are still with us.

When James VI lived in England, he said he governed Scotland by his pen.

According to legend, during the reign of James VI, Sawney Bean headed a clan of cannibal robbers living near Ballantrae.

Charles I became king in 1625. He had a lovely family and an even lovelier collection of paintings. Sadly, these didn't make him a good king.

He put off coming to Scotland to be crowned for eight years. The Scots felt he was ignoring them. They were even more annoyed when he tried to make their church more like the English one.

They set out their complaints in a National Covenant.

Charles took little notice, so the Scots rose in rebellion. Soon afterwards the English rebelled too and there was civil war in both Charles' kingdoms.

After a lot of bloodshed, Charles surrendered to the Scots. They handed him over to the English, who cut off his head. (It was sewn back on before he was buried.)

The Scots were so horrified by the execution of Charles I that they crowned his son Charles II. The English leader Oliver Cromwell was furious. He conquered Scotland and forced it to join with England. Charles II ran away to the Continent.

SAVING THE ROYAL HONOURS

Cromwell tried to steal the Crown Jewels but he was thwarted. They were hidden in a lobster pot and taken to safety.

Charles II eventually got his throne back, but did not return to Scotland. He stayed in England having a good time. Once again the Scots felt their king was ignoring them.

After Charles II died, his unpopular brother James VII, a Catholic, was driven 'over the water' (across the sea) to France. Those who wanted him back were known as Jacobites.

HOW THE JACOBITES SECRETLY TOASTED KING JAMES AFTER HE CROSSED THE SEA.

The English made sure Scottish merchants lost out to them. Many better-off Scots had lost a fortune on the Darien Scheme and decided that, if they couldn't beat the English, they might as well join them. So, pockets bulging with English bribes, in 1707, the Scottish parliament sadly voted for the two countries to become one.

Union with England was not popular, particularly in the Highlands. Twice, in 1715 and 1745, the exiled Stewarts came to take back their crown. The first attempt was a complete flop. But the '45 Rebellion, led by James VII's grandson Bonnie Prince Charlie, was not ...

The government made Highlanders stop wearing tartan and give up their weapons ... including the bagpipes. It said they were 'instruments of war'!

Things looked up a bit in 1773 when Scottish writer James Boswell helped launch the tourist industry. He took his English friend, Dr Samuel Johnson, on a tour of the Highlands and wrote a popular book about it.

THERE'S A NICE PLACE TO STAY, SAM

O.K. BUT NO MORE HAGGIS, PLEASE!

HERE! HERE!

After the Forty-Five, many Jacobites were executed or imprisoned. Many more were sent abroad or forced to join the British army. The Highlands suffered.

Meanwhile the Lowlands were buzzing with activity. Scots were on the make in banking and business. Others were writing, studying, painting and inventing, especially in Edinburgh.

The Carron Works, founded in 1759, was Scotland's first successful large scale iron works. Many famous generals would not go into battle without Carron artillery and cannonballs.

PEOPLE ALWAYS SEEM TO THINK I INVENTED THE STEAM ENGINE. I DIDN'T BUT I DID MAKE IT WORK BETTER ... MUCH BETTER!

TOP SCOT

JAMES WATT (1736–1819)

James Watt of Greenock made improvements to the steam engine so it could be used to power factory machinery, locomotives and ships. Before this the only engines had been water and wind mills. Watt's engine changed the world.

EDINBURGH CASTLE
The magnificent symbol of the Scottish nation – an odd mix of fortress, palace, prison, barracks, war memorial, museum and theatre.
ST GILES CATHEDRAL
The High Kirk of Edinburgh where Jenny Geddes cried 'May the Devil buckle your belly!' and threw her stool at the preacher for using Charles I's English-style prayer book.
ROYAL MILE
The 17th century writer Daniel Defoe called it 'the largest, longest and finest street ... in the world'.
WAVERLEY STATION
Opened in 1846 and named after Sir Walter Scott's novel.
UNIVERSITY
founded by James VI, as 'The Tounis' College, it has been teaching students since 1583.
HOW WOULD YOU LIKE TO TAKE PART IN A MEDICAL EXPERIMENT?
HOLYROOD PALACE
James IV, V and VI, Mary Queen of Scots, Charles I, Bonnie Prince Charlie and Queen Victoria all slept here.
BURKE AND HARE
Scotland's most famous criminals murdered 16 people by getting them drunk and suffocating them. They sold the bodies to the city's medical school.

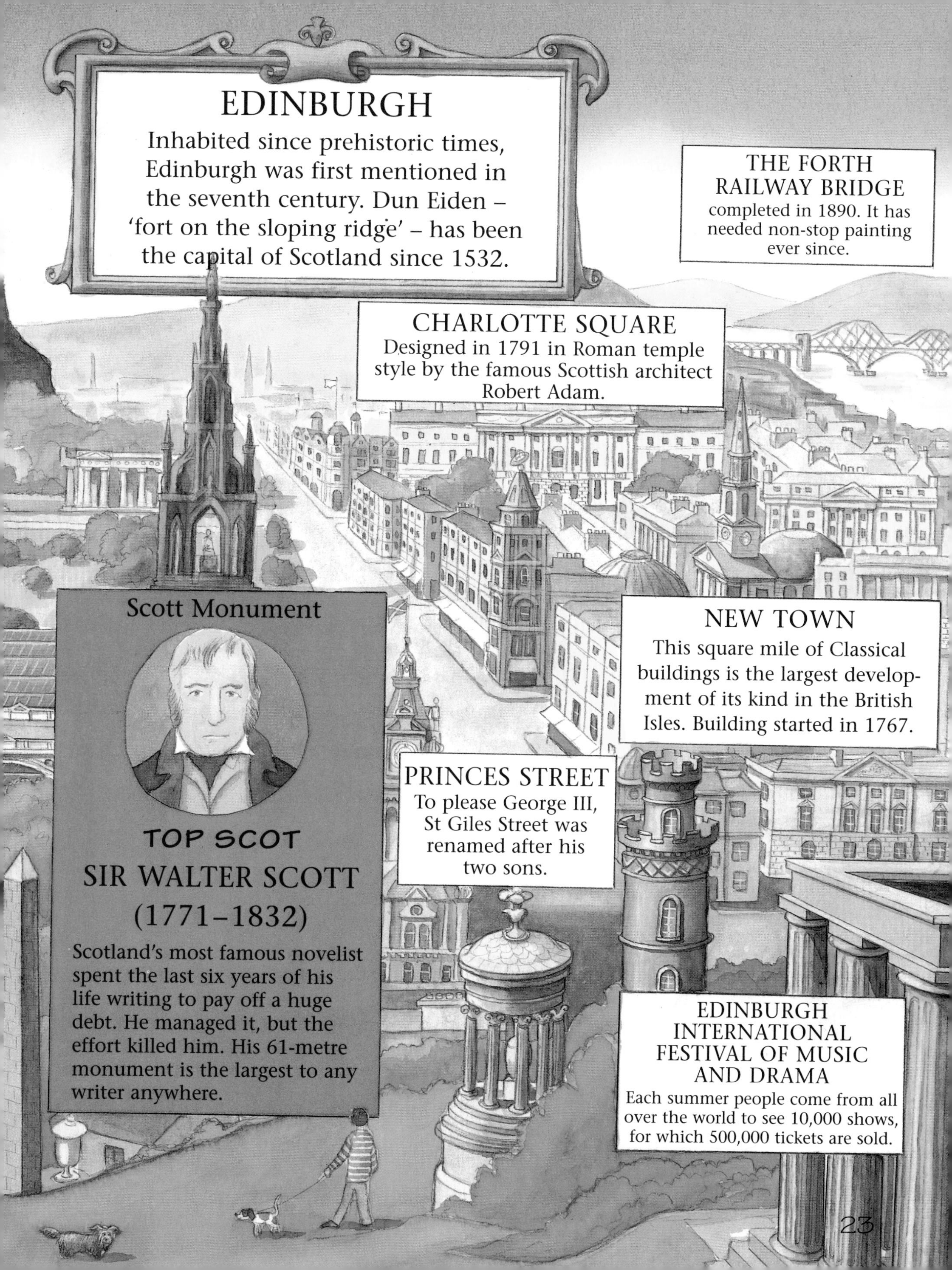

EDINBURGH

Inhabited since prehistoric times, Edinburgh was first mentioned in the seventh century. Dun Eiden – 'fort on the sloping ridge' – has been the capital of Scotland since 1532.

THE FORTH RAILWAY BRIDGE

completed in 1890. It has needed non-stop painting ever since.

CHARLOTTE SQUARE

Designed in 1791 in Roman temple style by the famous Scottish architect Robert Adam.

Scott Monument

TOP SCOT

SIR WALTER SCOTT (1771–1832)

Scotland's most famous novelist spent the last six years of his life writing to pay off a huge debt. He managed it, but the effort killed him. His 61-metre monument is the largest to any writer anywhere.

NEW TOWN

This square mile of Classical buildings is the largest development of its kind in the British Isles. Building started in 1767.

PRINCES STREET

To please George III, St Giles Street was renamed after his two sons.

EDINBURGH INTERNATIONAL FESTIVAL OF MUSIC AND DRAMA

Each summer people come from all over the world to see 10,000 shows, for which 500,000 tickets are sold.

Europe's first commercial steamship, the Comet, first puffed along the Clyde in 1812.

The horse-drawn Kilmarnock and Troon railway began carrying passengers in the same year.

In the Lowlands people were busier than ever, making things and selling them all over the world. A smoky, noisy belt of factories, mills, mines, warehouses, banks and dockyards sprang up around Edinburgh and Glasgow. Villages grew into towns, towns sprawled into cities. Canals and railways snaked across the countryside.

Some people made their fortunes. But many others had to live in slums amidst disease, dirt and pollution.

The New Lanark mill-owner Robert Owen saw that the happier his employees were, the harder they would work so he treated them well.

The Countess of Sutherland, a rich landowner, urged the young men who lived on her Highland estates to join the army. If they did not, she said, they would be replaced by sheep.

George IV's decision to wear Highland Dress on his 1822 visit to Scotland did more for the popularity of the garb than the monarch.

TOP SCOT

ROBBIE BURNS (1759–1796)

Scotland's favourite poet, who gave the world 'Auld Lang Syne', wrote hundreds of love songs in praise of his many bonnie lassies.

The Highlands were changing too. Grasping landowners cruelly cleared small farmers off the land to make way for sheep and deer. By 1850 the glens were almost deserted. Crumbling cottages were all that remained of the old way of life.

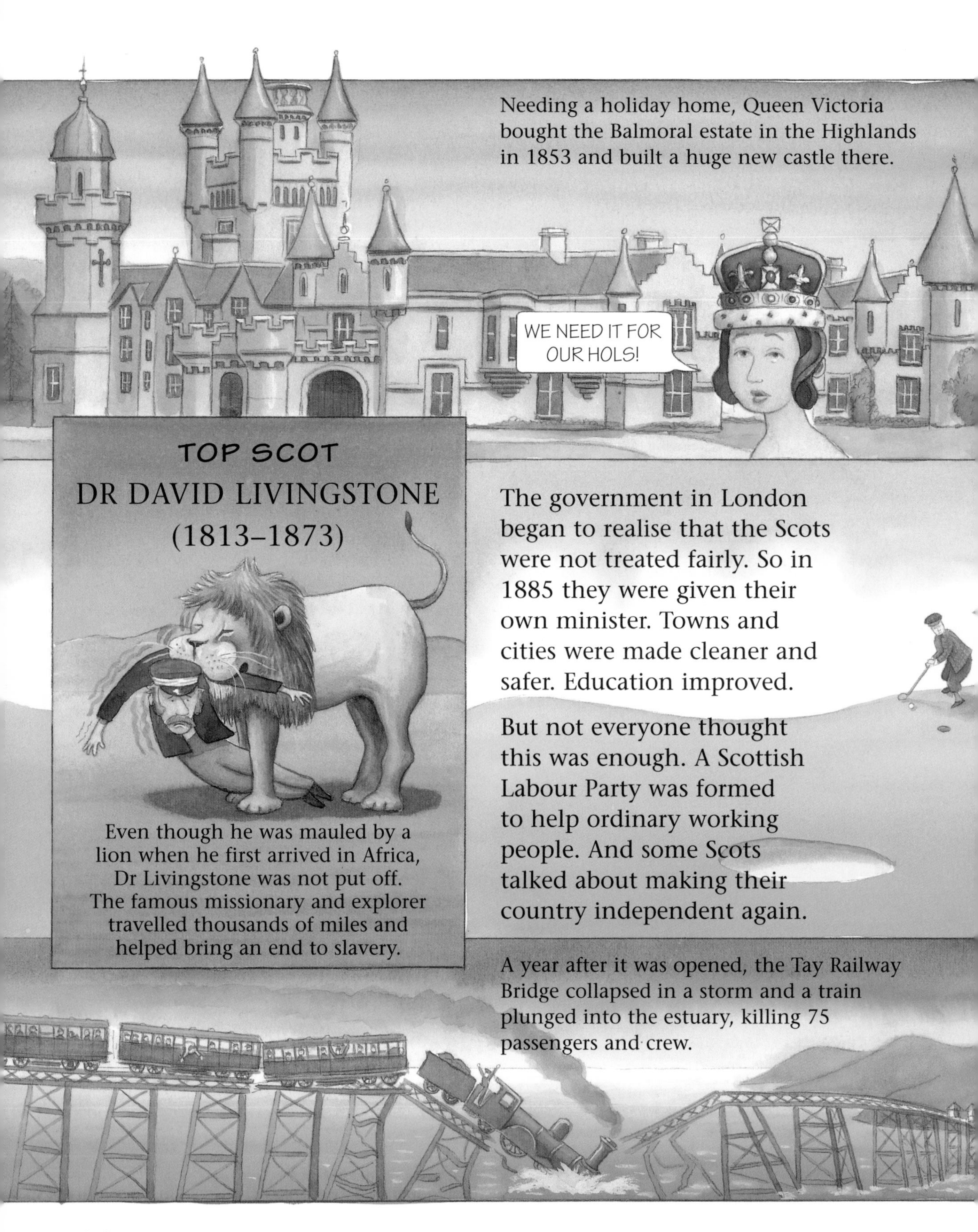

Needing a holiday home, Queen Victoria bought the Balmoral estate in the Highlands in 1853 and built a huge new castle there.

TOP SCOT

DR DAVID LIVINGSTONE (1813–1873)

Even though he was mauled by a lion when he first arrived in Africa, Dr Livingstone was not put off. The famous missionary and explorer travelled thousands of miles and helped bring an end to slavery.

The government in London began to realise that the Scots were not treated fairly. So in 1885 they were given their own minister. Towns and cities were made cleaner and safer. Education improved.

But not everyone thought this was enough. A Scottish Labour Party was formed to help ordinary working people. And some Scots talked about making their country independent again.

A year after it was opened, the Tay Railway Bridge collapsed in a storm and a train plunged into the estuary, killing 75 passengers and crew.

The First Scottish Football Association Cup was won by Queen's Park in 1874.

Battles with the Auld Enemy were now fought on the sports field, not the battle-field. Scotland drew its first international football match with England, but beat them at rugby. And when it came to golf, the English didn't stand a chance!

TOP SCOT
KEIR HARDIE
(1836–1915)

Bearded Keir Hardie, the first ever Labour MP, complained bitterly that parliament was wasting time by discussing the birth of a royal baby.

SCOTLAND v ENGLAND

During World War I men and women earned high wages building ships. The naval bases Scapa Flow, Invergordon and Rosyth also brought money and jobs. But Scottish casualties on the battlefield were terribly high.

In 1919 the Germans scuttled their battle fleet at Scapa Flow, Orkney. Most of it is still there.

There were hard times after the war. Great ships like the Queen Mary and the Queen Elizabeth were still being built, but wages fell and many workers were without jobs.

World War II turned the country into a military camp. Germany's first air-raid on Britain targeted the Forth Bridge. Clydeside was blitzed in 1941.

TOP SCOT

JOHN LOGIE BAIRD (1888–1946)

Ex-soap manufacturer John Baird sent the world's first TV picture in 1924. It travelled a few feet across the attic where he lived. Having no money, he made his apparatus out of a washstand, a tea chest, a biscuit tin, cardboard, string, darning needles and sealing wax.

Many Scots looked eagerly to the Labour Party which promised to make life better and fairer for all.

Others thought Scotland should be an independent country again and the Scottish National Party got its first MP in 1945.

Scotch Whisky

500 years ago James IV took to drinking whisky. By 1950 it was being shipped all over the world and earning Scotland a lot of money.

SCOTLAND RULES O.K.?

The Scots had plenty of practice at government before they got their parliament back. Recent cabinets have been stuffed with them. Of Prime Ministers this century, four have been Scots. (*left*)

Harold Macmillan's grandfather was a Highland crofter and Tony Blair went to school in Edinburgh. (*right*)

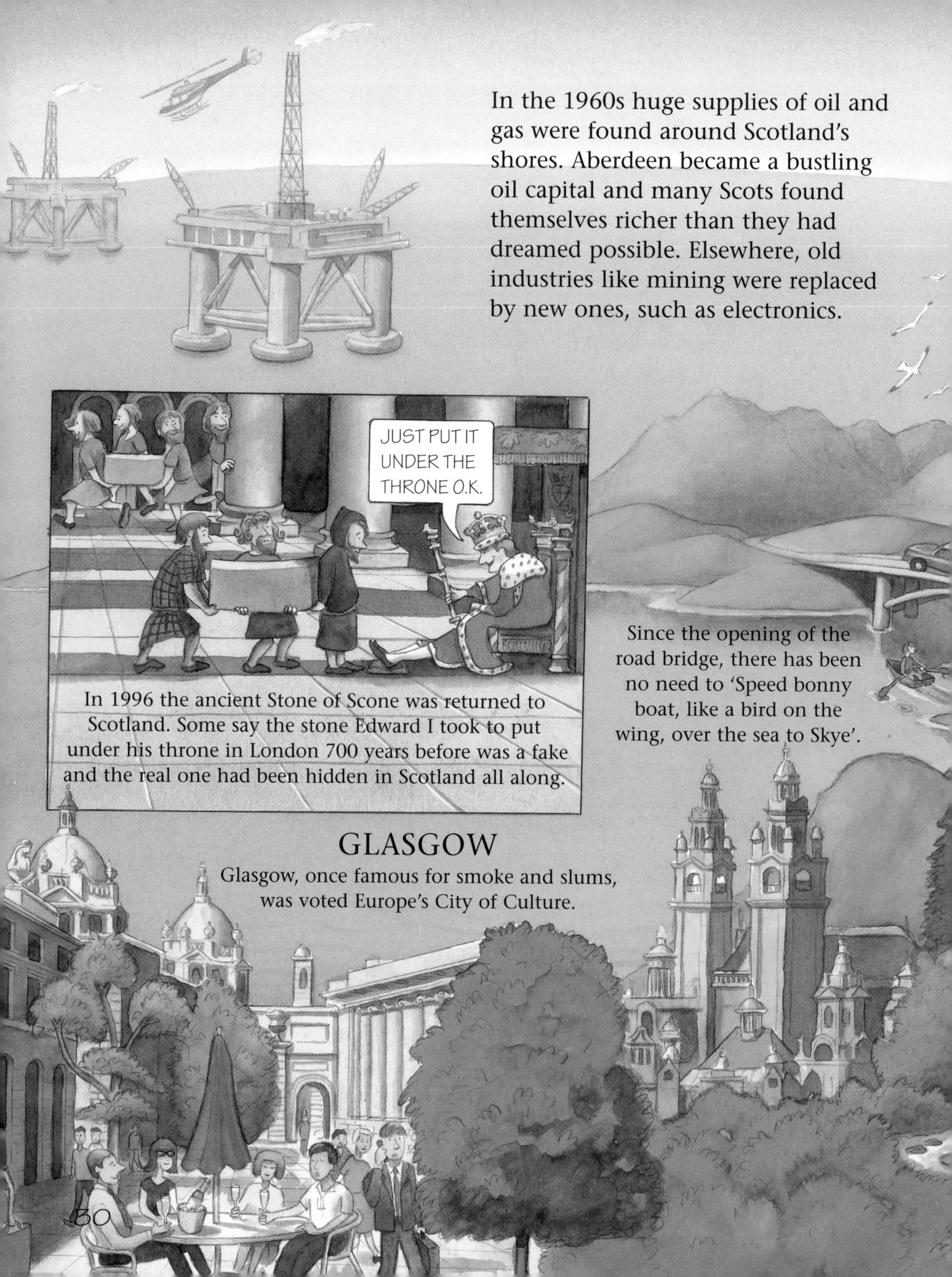

In the 1960s huge supplies of oil and gas were found around Scotland's shores. Aberdeen became a bustling oil capital and many Scots found themselves richer than they had dreamed possible. Elsewhere, old industries like mining were replaced by new ones, such as electronics.

In 1996 the ancient Stone of Scone was returned to Scotland. Some say the stone Edward I took to put under his throne in London 700 years before was a fake and the real one had been hidden in Scotland all along.

Since the opening of the road bridge, there has been no need to 'Speed bonny boat, like a bird on the wing, over the sea to Skye'.

GLASGOW

Glasgow, once famous for smoke and slums, was voted Europe's City of Culture.

After the ban on tartan was lifted in 1782, tartan kilts soon became the national dress.

Millions of tourists flocked to enjoy the country's culture and scenery. Edinburgh started its festival. Highlanders took to skiing.

The face of Scotland was changing so fast that from time to time the Loch Ness Monster rose from the waters to see what was going on.

In the 1820s people began seeing Highland life as romantic and Highland Games, including the famous tossing the caber, were started. Today the Games are a major tourist attraction.

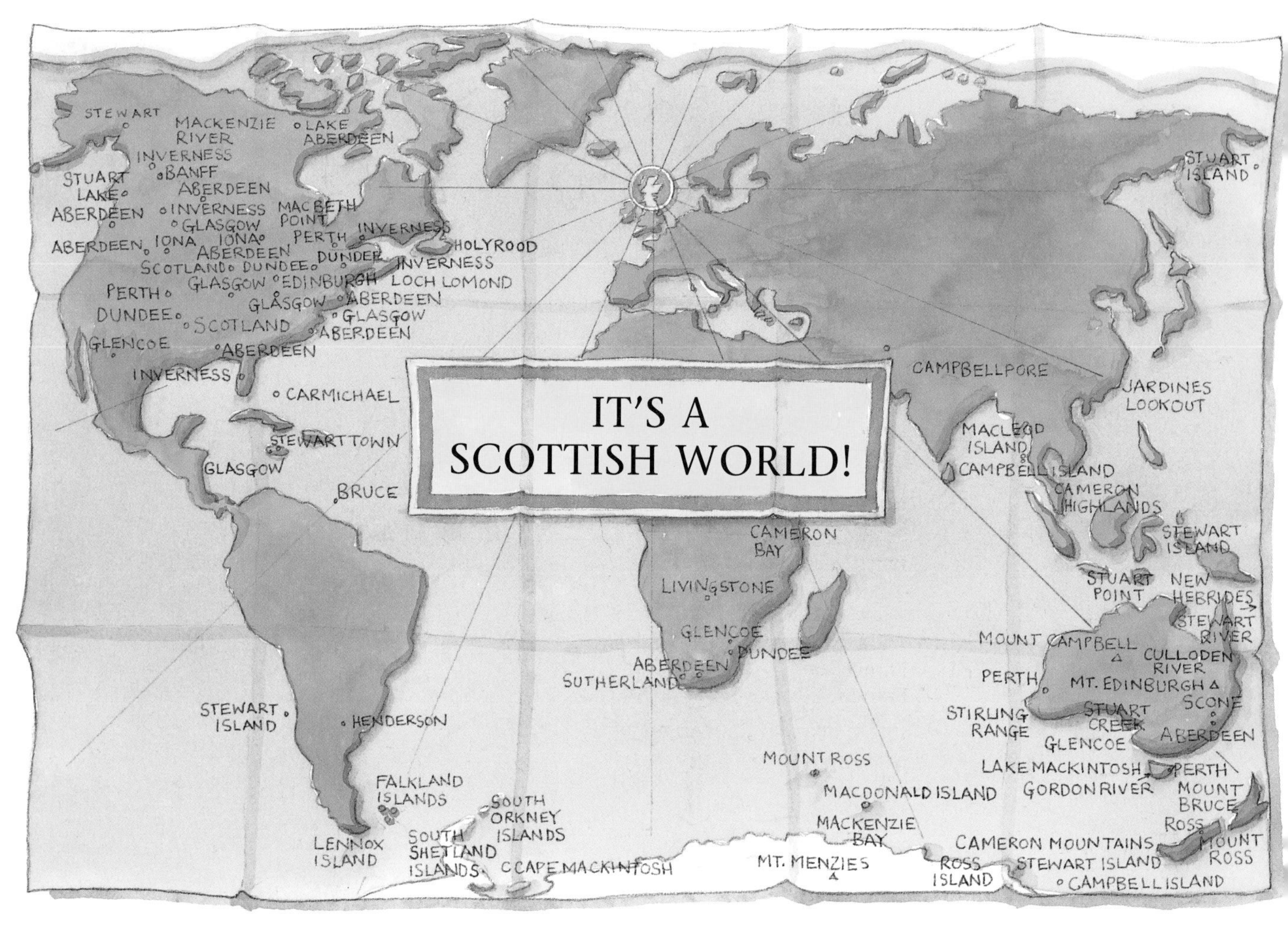

Scottish people have settled all over the world. Wherever they went, they took with them their clan names and the names of longed-for places back in Scotland. Telephone directories in Australia, Canada and the United States are full of MacDonalds, Campbells, Bruces and Stewarts.

No people are prouder of their native land than the Scots, wherever they may live. In 1997 the London government finally realised this and asked the Scots whether they wanted their parliament back. The answer: A resounding ...

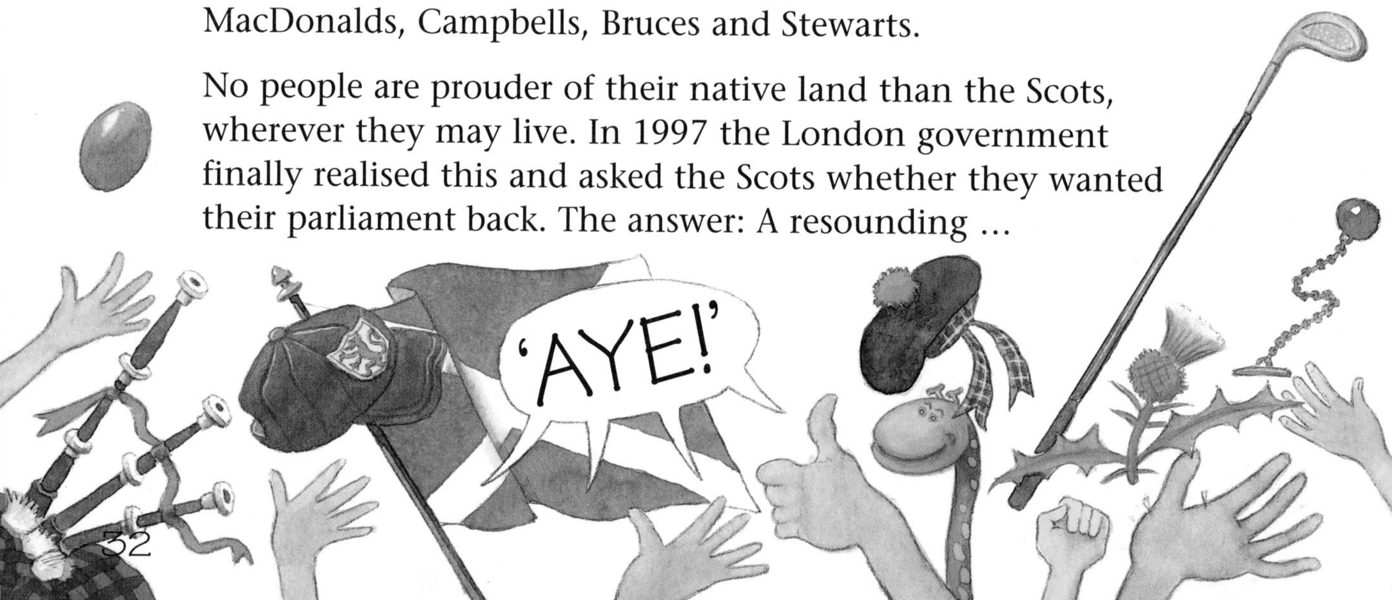

INDEX

OUTER HEBRIDES
STONE CIRCLE CALLANISH, LEWIS
FLORA MACDONALD TAKES BONNIE PRINCE CHARLIE FROM BENBECULA TO SKYE
BOSWELL AND JOHNSON ON SKYE
IONA THE OLD ABBEY FOUNDED BY ST COLUMBA
GLENFINNAN WHERE BONNIE PRINCE CHARLIE RAISED HIS STANDARD
LOCH NESS
BEN NEVIS
GLEN COE WHERE THE MACDONALDS WERE MASSACRED
WHISKY
ISLAY
WALLACE MONUMENT
GLASGOW
STIRLING CASTLE